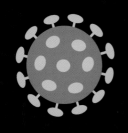

ATTACK OF THE...

VULGAR
VIRUSES

By William Anthony

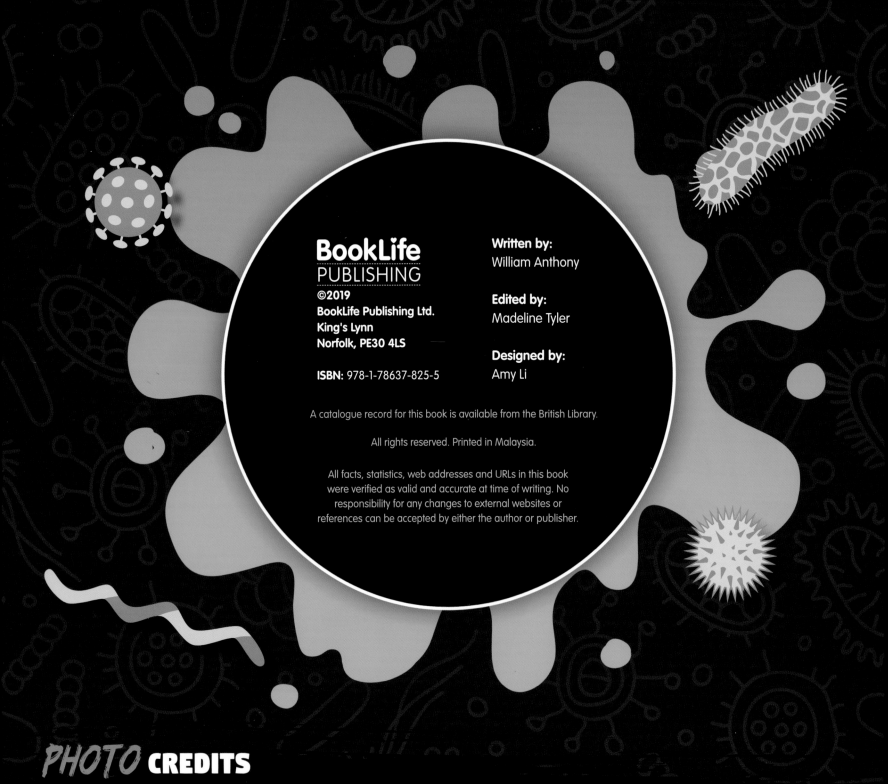

BookLife
PUBLISHING

©2019
BookLife Publishing Ltd.
King's Lynn
Norfolk, PE30 4LS

ISBN: 978-1-78637-825-5

Written by:
William Anthony

Edited by:
Madeline Tyler

Designed by:
Amy Li

A catalogue record for this book is available from the British Library.

All facts, statistics, web addresses and URLs in this book were verified as valid and accurate at time of writing. No responsibility for any changes to external websites or references can be accepted by either the author or publisher.

PHOTO CREDITS

All images courtesy of Shutterstock. With thanks to Getty Images, Thinkstock Photo and iStockphoto.

Used throughout (including cover) – chekart (background), Sonechko57 (slime), VectorShow (microbe characters), Alena Ohneva (vector microbes), Olga_C (circle image frame). Used throughout (excluding cover) – Photo Melon (clipboard), Lorelyn Medina (scientist characters). P4–5 – Imagerist, Naeblys, p6–7 – ASDF_MEDIA, Peeradach R, p8–9 – svtdesign, antpkr, ranjith ravindran, p10–11 – pornpan chaiu-dom, MaryValery, p12–13 – Marcel Jancovic, Dermatology11, Real Illusion, p14–15 – What's My Name, nobeastoffierce, VectorShow, p16–17 – Arit FongFung, MTPhoto_Life, p18–19 – MaryAnne Campbell, Svineyard, p20–21 – pinkeyes, wavebreakmedia, p22–23 – didesigns021, Africa Studio.

CONTENTS

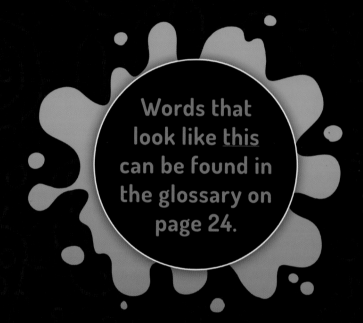

Words that look like <u>this</u> can be found in the glossary on page 24.

TRICKY WORDS

VIRUS = singular (one virus)
VIRUSES = plural (many viruses)
VIRAL = to do with one virus or many viruses

MINI MONSTERS

Look around you. What's the smallest thing you can see? Did you know there are thousands of smaller things you can't see? Some of them are microorganisms.

" Micro means tiny.
Organism means a living thing. "

Microorganisms are sometimes called microbes, and they are everywhere. They're on the floor, our desks and our clothes. They even live on our skin and in our bodies.

OH NO!

Get the <u>microscope</u>! These things do not sound good!

VULGAR VIRUSES

Viruses are a type of microbe. Like other microbes, they are too small to see. Viruses can cause bad things to happen if they get inside our bodies.

"Bad things? How bad? Can we hide from them?"

Viruses take over the <u>cells</u> of living things. Scientists can't decide whether viruses are alive or not.

If we can't even decide if viruses are alive or not, how are we ever going to fight back?

Viruses can <u>spread</u> in lots of different ways. They can be spread by:

- Coughing
- Sneezing
- Touching other people
- Touching things without washing your hands afterwards

"Everybody GET BACK!"

We can't treat viral <u>infections</u> in the same way that we treat other infections. <u>Antibiotics</u> don't work on viruses.

They don't? Does that mean the viruses can just run wild?

NOROVIRUS

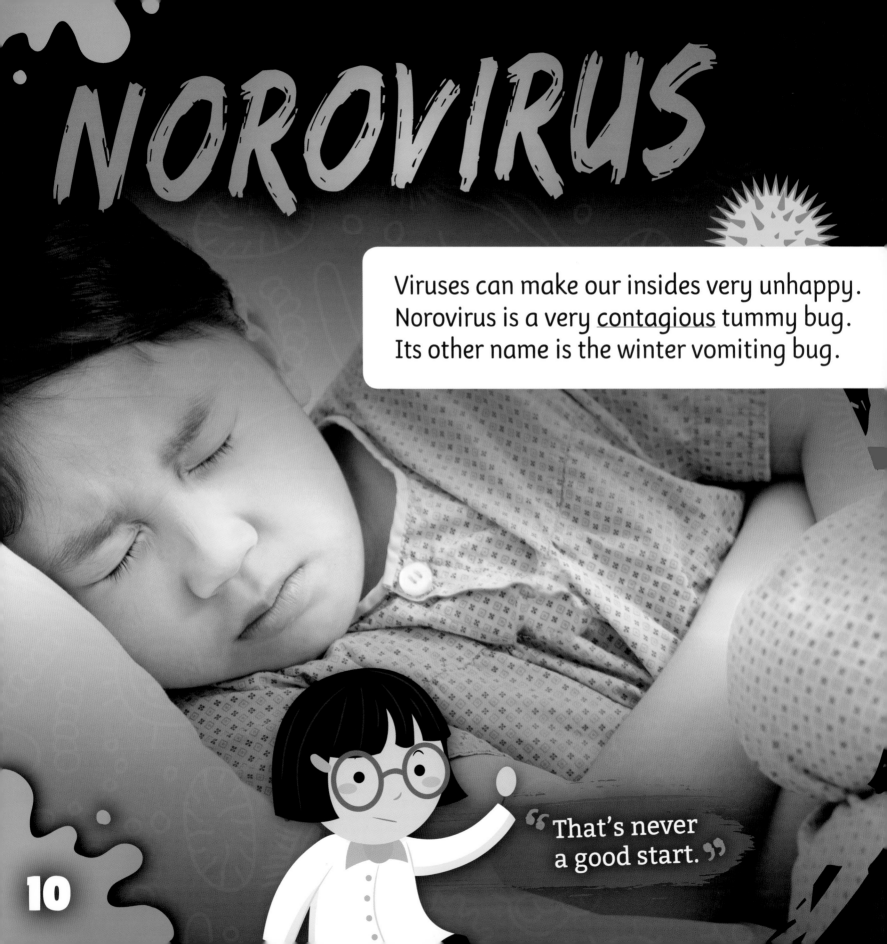

Viruses can make our insides very unhappy. Norovirus is a very <u>contagious</u> tummy bug. Its other name is the winter vomiting bug.

"That's never a good start."

The effects of norovirus definitely aren't pretty. They include:

- Vomiting
- More vomiting
- Diarrhoea (runny poo)
- A lot more vomiting

ARGH!
I feel sick and I haven't even got norovirus!

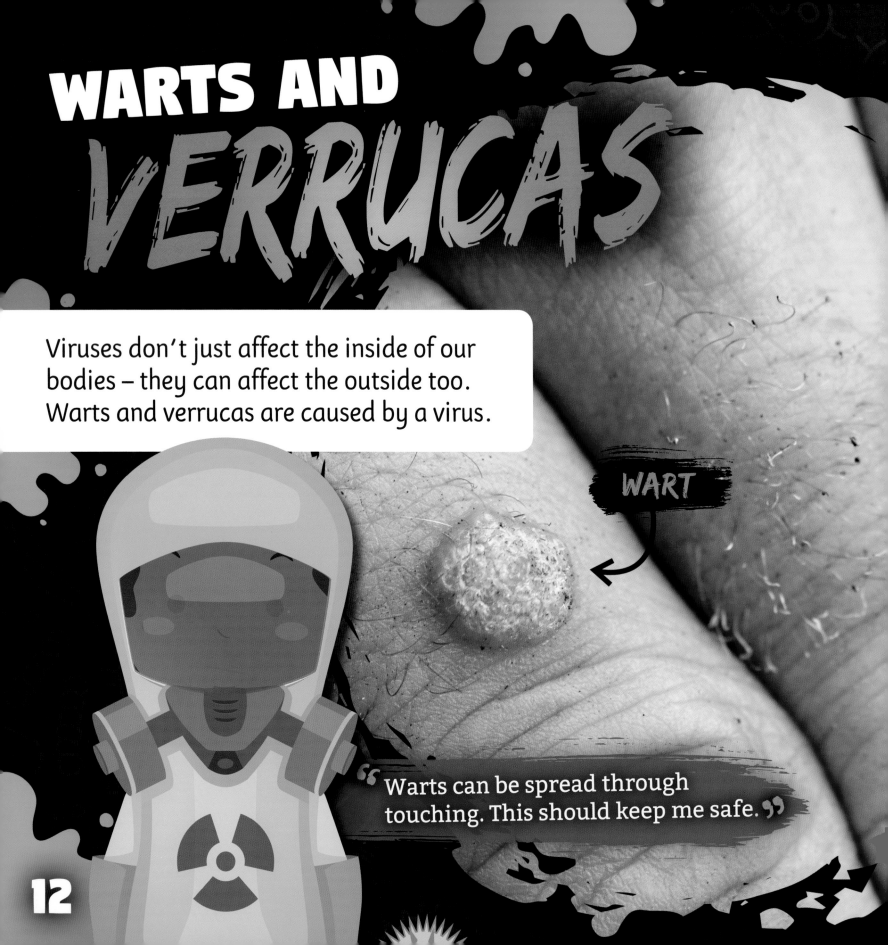

WARTS AND VERRUCAS

Viruses don't just affect the inside of our bodies – they can affect the outside too. Warts and verrucas are caused by a virus.

WART

Warts can be spread through touching. This should keep me safe.

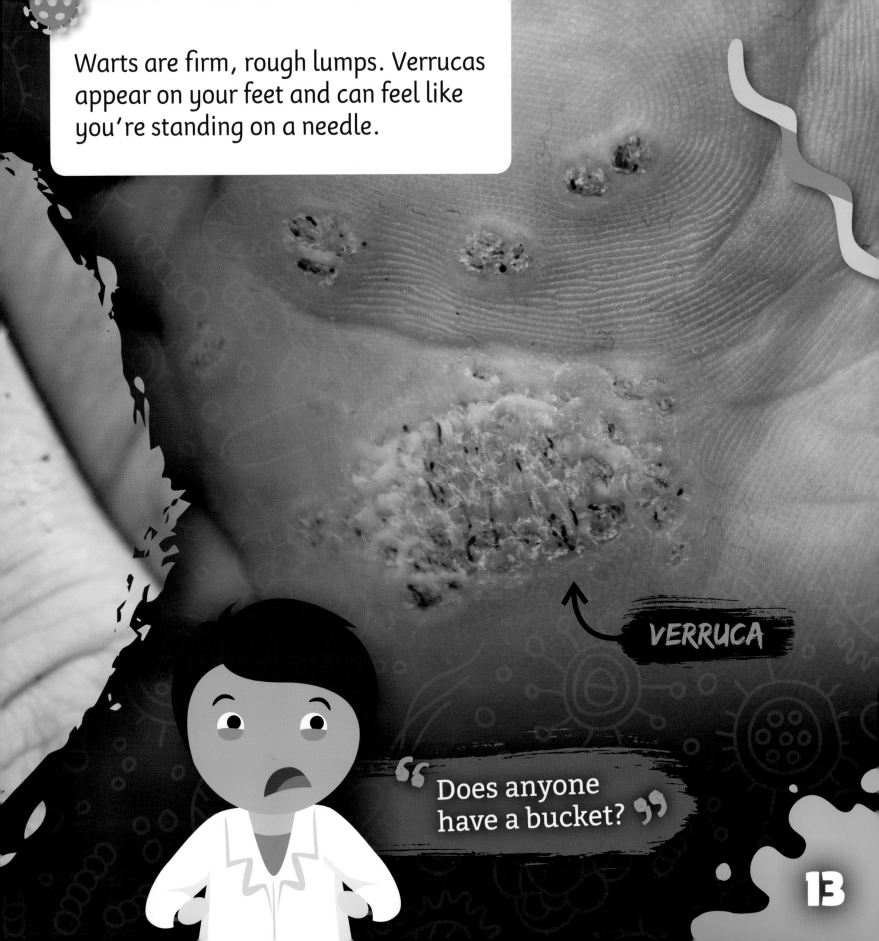

Warts are firm, rough lumps. Verrucas appear on your feet and can feel like you're standing on a needle.

VERRUCA

"Does anyone have a bucket?"

RABIES

Viruses can <u>invade</u> animals and make them very ill. Rabies is a dangerous virus that can be spread by the spit of <u>infected</u> animals.

RABIES VIRUS

"The viruses are attacking animals? Somebody save us!"

Dogs can get rabies if they are bitten by another animal that has it. Rabies can cause:

- Unusual anger
- High <u>temperature</u>
- Difficulty swallowing
- Difficulty moving

"Always tell an adult if your dog is acting strangely."

CHICKENPOX

Have you or any of your friends ever had a rash with lots of spots? It could be chickenpox. It's completely normal in children.

Relax!

Chickenpox usually goes away after two weeks, and most people never get it again.

Chickenpox might start like a normal cold, with lots of sneezing and coughing. After a few days, a rash starts. It's important not to scratch the spots.

ROSE ROSETTE

Viruses can attack almost any living thing, including plants. Rose rosette is a viral disease in rose plants.

"Not the beautiful roses!"

The disease is spread by <u>mites</u>. It causes parts of the plant to crinkle up and grow the wrong way. Most of the time, the virus kills the rose.

How are the viruses getting away with this?

19

FLU

One of the most common viral illnesses is flu. It is spread by the coughs and sneezes of people who have flu.

"Why does everything to do with viruses have to be gross?"

Flu can be very unpleasant. It can cause:

- High temperature
- Headache
- Coughing and sneezing
- Sore throat
- Aches
- Tiredness

"I'm sure someone told me that there's a <u>vaccine</u> for flu..."

STRIKING BACK

Viruses are not easy to treat, so we try to stop ourselves getting infected in the first place. Vaccines can help keep us safe from viruses.

> Vaccines might hurt for a second, but they help to keep us safe!

When we do get infected, there are some treatments we can use to help us with any <u>symptoms</u>. The fight against viruses has begun!

"This cream for my chickenpox is just what the doctor ordered – literally."

GLOSSARY

antibiotics	medicines that are used to kill harmful bacteria and cure infections
cells	the basic building blocks that make up all living things
contagious	able to spread from one person or animal to another
infected	when germs or disease have entered part of the body
infections	illnesses caused by dirt or microbes getting into the body
invade	to enter a body without being welcome or invited
microscope	a piece of scientific equipment that makes things look many times bigger
mites	very small creatures that often live on plants, animals, and food
spread	to move around from place to place to affect a larger area
symptoms	the signs of an illness
temperature	how hot or cold something or someone is
vaccine	medicine that is injected into a person or animal to protect against a disease

INDEX

24